The Web Development Starter Kit

Build Websites with HTML, CSS & JavaScript

Benjamin Evans

DEDICATION

To the relentless seekers of knowledge, the curious minds tirelessly decoding the mysteries of algorithms and code. This book is dedicated to you, the coders who embrace the challenges of neural networks with fervor and determination. May these pages serve as stepping stones on your journey, empowering you to unravel the complexities of this dynamic field and craft solutions that shape the future. Your passion fuels the innovation that drives our world forward, and for that, I extend my deepest gratitude and admiration.

CONTENTS

ACKNOWLEDGMENTS

I would like to extend my sincere gratitude to all those who have contributed to the realization of this book. First and foremost, I am indebted to my family for their unwavering support and encouragement throughout this endeavor. Their love and understanding have been my anchor in the stormy seas of writing.

I am deeply thankful to the experts whose guidance and insights have illuminated my path and enriched the content of this book. Their mentorship has been invaluable in shaping my understanding and refining my ideas.

I also extend my appreciation to those whose constructive feedback and insightful suggestions have helped polish this work to its finest form.

Furthermore, I am grateful to the countless individuals whose research, publications, and contributions have paved the way for the insights shared in these pages.

Last but not least, I express my heartfelt appreciation to the readers who embark on this journey with me. Your curiosity and engagement breathe life into these words, and it is for you that this book exists.

Thank you all for being part of this remarkable journey.

CHAPTER 1

Welcome to the exciting world of web development! In this chapter, we'll delve into the fundamentals, understand what web development entails, explore the essential components that make up a web page, discover the benefits of acquiring this valuable skill, and finally, set up your development environment to kickstart your learning journey.

1.1 What is Web Development?

Web development is the process of creating and maintaining websites. It encompasses a range of skills used to build user interfaces, define how information is displayed and accessed, and ensure websites function seamlessly across different devices.

Here's a breakdown of the core aspects of web development:

- **Front-End Development:** This focuses on the visual side of a website, crafting the user interface (UI) elements like buttons, menus, and text that users interact with directly. Languages like HTML, CSS, and JavaScript are the primary tools of front-end developers.

- **Back-End Development:** This works behind the scenes, handling tasks like storing and managing data, processing user requests, and ensuring website functionality. Languages like Python, Java, and PHP are commonly used for back-end development.

- **Full-Stack Development:** This encompasses both front-end and back-end development, making the developer a jack-of-all-trades who can handle all aspects of website creation.

1.2 The Building Blocks of a Web Page

Every website you visit is built using a combination of essential elements.

- **HTML (HyperText Markup Language):** This is the foundation of any web page. It acts like a blueprint, defining the structure and content of a page using tags. These tags tell the web browser how to display different elements like headings, paragraphs, images, and more. **(Code Snippet Example:** ```html <!DOCTYPE html> <html> <head> <title>My First Web Page</title> </head> <body> <h1>Welcome to My Website!</h1> <p>This is a simple paragraph.</p> </body> </html>

Code snippet

CSS (Cascading Style Sheets): While HTML defines the structure, CSS dictates how the content is styled. It allows you to control the appearance of your webpage elements such as font size, colors, backgrounds, and layout. (**Code Snippet Example: ```css

```css
body {
  font-family: Arial, sans-serif;
  background-color: #f0f0f0;
}

h1 {
  color: #333;
  text-align: center;
}
```
)

JavaScript: This is a scripting language that adds interactivity and dynamism to web pages. It allows you to create animations, respond to user actions (like clicking a button), and manipulate the content of a page without requiring a complete page reload. (**Code Snippet Example: ```javascript

```javascript
function changeColor() {
  const element = document.getElementById("text");
  element.style.color = "red";
}
```

```
```)
```

## Understanding the Relationship:

These three elements work together in a beautiful dance to bring a website to life. Imagine HTML as the skeleton providing the basic structure, CSS as the clothing that styles the skeleton, and JavaScript as the personality that brings movement and interaction.

## 1.3 Benefits of Learning Web Development

Web development is a highly sought-after skill with numerous advantages:

**High Demand:** Web developers are in constant demand as the online world continues to expand. Companies across industries need websites, and skilled developers are crucial for building and maintaining them.

**Creative Outlet:** Web development allows you to express your creativity by designing and building visually
```

appealing and user-friendly websites. You can experiment with layouts, color schemes, and interactive elements to create unique online experiences.

Problem-Solving Skills: Web development involves solving problems, both technical and logical, in order to achieve desired website functionality. You'll learn to debug code, find solutions to errors, and optimize performance, enhancing your problem-solving skills valuable in various aspects of life.

Career Opportunities: Mastering web development opens doors to various career paths, from freelance work to agency positions and in-house development teams. You can choose a career path that aligns with your interests and goals.

Marketable Skill: Web development expertise is valuable in today's job market, especially with the increasing reliance on online presence across industries. Having this skill set makes you a more competitive candidate in the job market.

Personal Projects: The skills you learn can be used to build your own personal projects, online portfolios, or even blogs. This allows you to showcase your creativity and technical abilities to potential employers or even blogs. This allows you to showcase your creativity and technical abilities to potential employers or clients. Web development empowers you to build your online presence and brand on your own terms.

1.4 Setting Up Your Development Environment

Before embarking on your coding adventures, you'll need a development environment. This consists of the software tools you'll use to write, edit, and test your code. Here's a basic setup:

- **Text Editor:** A basic text editor like Notepad (Windows) or TextEdit (Mac) allows you to write your code. However, for a more feature-rich experience, consider using a code editor specifically designed for web development. Popular options include:

○ **Visual Studio Code:** A free, open-source code editor with extensive features like syntax highlighting, code completion, debugging tools, and built-in support for various programming languages. It's a popular choice for beginners and experienced developers alike.

○ **Sublime Text:** Another popular code editor with a clean interface and extensive customization options. It offers various plugins specifically suited for web development tasks. While it has a free trial, it requires a license for continued use.

○ **Atom:** An open-source code editor known for its user-friendly interface and hackable nature. It allows for extensive customization through themes and packages, making it a good option for developers who prefer a highly personalized workspace.

These code editors provide features that make coding more efficient and enjoyable. Syntax highlighting helps you differentiate between code elements like keywords and variable names, making your code easier to read. Code completion suggests code snippets as you type, saving you time and reducing errors. Debugging tools help you identify and fix errors in your code.

- **Web Browser:** This is where you'll see your website come to life. Every web browser interprets HTML, CSS, and JavaScript code and displays the webpage accordingly. Popular web browsers include Google Chrome, Mozilla Firefox, Apple Safari, and Microsoft Edge. It's recommended to have at least a couple of these browsers installed on your system to ensure your website renders consistently across different platforms.

Additional Tips:

- **Live Server Extensions:** Consider installing a live

server extension for your code editor. This allows you to run your HTML and CSS code directly in the editor, providing a real-time preview of your webpage as you make changes, streamlining the development process. Popular live server extensions include Live Server for Visual Studio Code and Brackets Live Preview.

- **Sample Code and Tutorials:** There are numerous online resources available to help you learn web development. Websites like W3Schools (https://www.w3schools.com/), Mozilla Developer Network (MDN) (https://developer.mozilla.org/en-US/), and freeCodeCamp (https://www.freecodecamp.org/) offer tutorials, code examples, and interactive exercises to get you started.

By setting up your development environment and utilizing the available resources, you'll be well-equipped to embark on your web development journey!

CHAPTER 2

DEMYSTIFYING HTML

Welcome to the exciting world of HTML! we'll delve into the foundational language of the web – HyperText Markup Language (HTML). We'll explore what HTML is, understand its basic structure, dive into essential tags used for building web pages, and finally, guide you through creating your very first webpage!

2.1 What is HTML?

HTML is not a programming language, but a markup language. It uses a system of tags to define the structure and content of a web page. These tags tell the web browser how to display different elements, like headings, paragraphs, images, and more. Think of HTML as the blueprint of your webpage, outlining the layout and organization of the content.

Here's an analogy: Imagine building a house. Bricks are the building blocks, but you need a blueprint to determine where those bricks go, how they connect, and what rooms they form. Similarly, HTML acts as the blueprint for your webpage, defining the structure and organization of the content displayed by the web browser.

2.2 Basic HTML Structure

Every HTML document follows a specific structure. Here's a breakdown of the key components:

- **DOCTYPE Declaration:** This line at the very beginning specifies the document type as HTML.

HTML

```
<!DOCTYPE html>
```

- **HTML Tag:** This is the root element that encloses the entire HTML document.

HTML

```
<html>
 ... (Your HTML content goes here)
</html>
```

- **Head Section:** This section contains information about the document itself, but is not displayed on the webpage. It typically includes the page title and meta information.

HTML

```
<head>
 <title>My First Web Page</title>
</head>
```

- **Body Section:** This section contains the visible content of your webpage, including headings, paragraphs, images, links, and other elements.

HTML

```
<body>
 <h1>Welcome to My Website!</h1>
 <p>This is a paragraph.</p>
</body>
```

Remember: Every opening tag (<tag>) should have a corresponding closing tag (</tag>) to properly define the element.

2.3 Essential HTML Tags

Now, let's explore some fundamental HTML tags you'll use to build your webpages:

- **Heading Tags (h1 - h6):** These tags define headings of different sizes. <h1> creates the largest heading, while <h6> creates the smallest.

HTML

```
<h1>This is a Heading 1</h1>
<h2>This is a Heading 2</h2>
<h3>This is a Heading 3</h3>
```

- **Paragraph Tag (<p>):** This tag defines a paragraph of text.

HTML

```
<p>This is a paragraph of text. You can add multiple
```

paragraphs to your webpage.</p>

- **Line Break Tag** (<br>): This inserts a line break within a paragraph, moving the text to the next line without creating a new paragraph.

HTML

This text is on the first line
This text is on the second line

- **Image Tag** (<img>**): This tag displays an image on your webpage. You need to specify the source (src`) of the image file.

HTML

<img src="image.jpg" alt="Description of the image">

- The alt attribute is important for accessibility, providing a text description of the image for users who cannot see it.
- **Link Tag** (<a>): This tag creates a hyperlink that, when clicked, directs the user to another webpage or a specific location on the same page.

HTML

<a   href="https://www.example.com">Visit   Example Website</a>

- The href attribute specifies the destination URL of the link.

These are just a few essential tags to get you started. As you progress, you'll discover a vast array of HTML tags to build more complex and interactive webpages.

2.4 Building Your First Web Page

Now that you're equipped with the basics, let's create your first webpage! Here's a step-by-step guide:

1. **Open a text editor:** Choose a text editor like Notepad (Windows) or TextEdit (Mac). For a more user-friendly experience with code highlighting, consider using a code editor like Visual Studio Code.
2. **Start with the basic structure:** Paste the following code into your editor:

HTML

```
<!DOCTYPE html>
<html>
<head>
  <title>My First Web Page</title>
</head>
<body>
  <h1>Welcome to My Website!</h1>
    <p>This is my first webpage. I'm excited to learn more
about HTML and build amazing websites!</p>
    <img src="website_logo.png" alt="Website Logo">
</body>
</html>
```

3. **Save the file:** Save the code you pasted as an HTML file. You can name it something like "index.html".

4. **Open the file in a web browser:** Double-click the saved HTML file to open it in your default web browser. You should see your first webpage displayed with the title "My First Web Page," a heading, a paragraph, and an image (if you have a

"website_logo.png" file in the same location).

Congratulations! You've successfully created your first webpage using HTML. This is just the beginning of your web development journey. As you explore further, you'll discover more tags to style your webpage with CSS and add interactivity with JavaScript.

Additional Tips:

- **Experiment with different tags:** Try adding more headings, paragraphs, and images to your webpage. Play around with the structure to see how it affects the layout.

- **Validate your code:** There are online tools available to validate your HTML code and ensure it's properly structured. This helps catch any errors you might have made. Websites like W3C Markup Validation Service (https://validator.w3.org/) offer free HTML validation.

- **Explore online resources:** Numerous online

tutorials and resources can guide you further in your HTML learning journey. Websites like W3Schools (https://www.w3schools.com/html/), Mozilla Developer Network (MDN) (https://developer.mozilla.org/en-US/docs/Web/HTML), and freeCodeCamp ([invalid URL removed]) offer comprehensive guides and interactive exercises to solidify your understanding.

By following these steps and exploring available resources, you'll be well on your way to mastering the fundamentals of HTML and building more complex and creative web pages!

CHAPTER 3

Diving Deeper into HTML

Let's explore more elements to enhance your webpages. This will cover advanced formatting options, creating hyperlinks, understanding semantic HTML, and even building interactive forms.

3.1 Working with Headings, Paragraphs, and Lists

We explored basic headings (<h1> to <h6>) and paragraphs (<p>) in Chapter 2. Now, let's see how you can format these elements further:

- **Heading Styles:** While headings (<h1> to <h6>) define the size hierarchy, you can also add additional styling using the class attribute. This allows you to customize the font, color, or other visual aspects of your headings.

HTML

```
<h1 class="main-heading">Welcome to My Website!</h1>
<p>This is a paragraph with a <span class="highlight">highlighted text</span>.</p>
```

- In this example, the class="main-heading" attribute applied to the <h1> tag allows you to define specific styles for the main heading in your CSS (covered later). Similarly, the <span> tag with class="highlight" creates a styled inline element within the paragraph.

- **Line Breaks and Paragraph Breaks:** We previously saw the <br> tag for line breaks within a paragraph. To create a new paragraph visually without adding extra space in the HTML code, use the <p> tag with a closing tag (</p>).

- **Unordered Lists (<ul>) and Ordered Lists (<ol>):**

These tags create bulleted (<ul>) or numbered (<ol>) lists. Each list item is defined using the <li> tag.

HTML

```
<ul>
 <li>Item 1</li>
 <li>Item 2</li>
 <li>Item 3</li>
</ul>
<ol>
 <li>Step 1</li>
 <li>Step 2</li>
 <li>Step 3</li>
</ol>
```

- **Nesting Lists:** You can create nested lists to create more complex structures.

HTML

```
<ul>
 <li>Item 1</li>
 <li>Item 2
  <ul>
   <li>Sub-item 2.1</li>
   <li>Sub-item 2.2</li>
```

```
  </ul>
  </li>
  <li>Item 3</li>
  </ul>
```

3.2 Creating Links and Images

You learned about creating hyperlinks with the <a> tag in Chapter 2. Here's a deeper look:

- **Link Attributes:** The <a> tag has various attributes that define the link's behavior:
  - href: This is the most crucial attribute, specifying the destination URL the link points to.
  - title: This attribute provides a tooltip that appears when hovering over the link, offering additional information.
  - target: This attribute defines how the linked content opens. For example, target="_blank" opens the link in a new tab.

HTML

```
<a      href="https://www.example.com"      title="Visit
Example Website">Example Website</a>
```

- **Images:** We covered the basic image tag (<img>) previously. Here are some additional points:
    - width and height attributes: These define the dimensions of the image displayed on the webpage. It's recommended to specify these attributes to avoid layout issues.
    - alt attribute (remember this from Chapter 2?): This is crucial for accessibility, providing a text description of the image for users who cannot see it.

HTML

```
<img src="image.jpg" alt="Description of the image"
width="300" height="200">
```

3.3 Understanding Semantic HTML

Semantic HTML focuses on using tags that describe the

meaning and purpose of the content, rather than just its appearance. This improves accessibility, search engine optimization (SEO), and overall code readability.

Here are some examples of semantic tags:

- <h1> to <h6> for headings (already covered)
- <header> for the header section of a webpage
- <nav> for navigation menus
- <section> for distinct sections of content
- <article> for self-contained pieces of content (like blog posts)
- <aside> for content that is indirectly related to the main content (like sidebars)

Using semantic tags not only improves the structure of your webpage but also conveys meaning to assistive technologies used by people with disabilities. Screen readers, for example, can interpret the content structure based on semantic tags, providing a better user experience.

Here's an example comparing a non-semantic approach

with a semantic approach:

Non-Semantic:

HTML

```
<div id="header">
  <h1>Welcome to My Website!</h1>
  <nav>
   <ul>
     <li><a href="#">Home</a></li>
     <li><a href="#">About</a></li>
     <li><a href="#">Contact</a></li>
   </ul>
  </nav>
</div>
```

Semantic:

HTML

```
<header>
  <h1>Welcome to My Website!</h1>
  <nav>
   <ul>
     <li><a href="#">Home</a></li>
     <li><a href="#">About</a></li>
     <li><a href="#">Contact</a></li>
   </ul>
  </nav>
</div>
```

In the semantic example, the <header> and <nav> tags clearly define the purpose of those sections, making the code more readable and maintainable.

3.4 Building Interactive Forms

HTML forms allow users to interact with your webpage by submitting information. Here's a breakdown of essential form elements:

- **Form Tag** (<form>)**:** This tag defines the beginning and end of a form. It has an essential attribute action that specifies the URL where the form data will be submitted.

- **Form Elements:** Various elements can be included within the <form> tags to capture user input:

  - **Text Input** (<input type="text">)**:** Creates a single-line text field for users to enter text.

- ○ **Password Input** (<input type="password">**):** Similar to text input, but hides the characters as the user types for password security.

- ○ **Radio Buttons** (<input type="radio">**):** Used to create a group of options where only one selection can be made.

- ○ **Checkboxes** (<input type="checkbox">**):** Allow users to select multiple options from a set.

- ○ **Textarea** (<textarea>**):** Creates a multi-line text input field for users to enter longer text.

- ○ **Submit Button** (<input type="submit">**):** When clicked, submits the form data to the specified URL (defined in the <form> tag).

Here's a basic example of a contact form:

HTML

```
<form action="/submit_form.php" method="post">
  <label for="name">Name:</label>
  <input type="text" id="name" name="name" required>
  <br>
```

```
<label for="email">Email:</label>
    <input type="email" id="email" name="email"
required>
    <br>
    <label for="message">Message:</label>
        <textarea id="message" name="message"
required></textarea>
    <br>
    <input type="submit" value="Submit">
</form>
```

Note: This is a simplified example. Processing form data typically involves server-side scripting languages like PHP or Python, which is beyond the scope of this chapter on HTML.

By incorporating these elements, you can create user-friendly forms to gather information, feedback, or even process orders on your webpage.

This chapter explored various ways to enhance your webpages using HTML. You learned advanced formatting techniques, explored creating interactive elements like links and forms, and delved into the importance of semantic HTML. As you continue your web development journey, remember to practice and experiment with these concepts to build more engaging and informative webpages.

CHAPTER 4

Introduction to CSS

Having mastered the fundamentals of HTML, you're now ready to explore the world of CSS (Cascading Style Sheets)! CSS is the magic wand that transforms your basic HTML structure into visually appealing and well-designed webpages.

4.1 What is CSS and Why is it Important?

Imagine building a house. While the blueprint (HTML) defines the structure, you wouldn't want to live in a bare-bones frame. That's where CSS comes in – it acts like the interior designer, adding style, color, and layout to your webpage.

Here's what CSS offers:

- **Separation of Concerns:** Separating HTML (content) from CSS (style) promotes better code organization and maintainability. You can modify the appearance of your webpage without altering the underlying content structure.

- **Consistent Design:** CSS allows you to define styles once and apply them to multiple elements throughout your webpage, ensuring a consistent and cohesive visual experience.

- **Improved User Experience:** By controlling the visual presentation, you can enhance readability, usability, and overall user experience of your webpage.

- **Responsive Design:** CSS plays a crucial role in creating responsive webpages that adapt their layout to different screen sizes, ensuring a seamless experience on desktops, tablets, and mobile devices.

4.2 Selectors: Targeting Elements on Your Page

CSS uses selectors to target specific elements on your webpage and apply styles to them. Here are some fundamental selectors:

- **Element Selector:** Targets an HTML element by its tag name. For example, h1 { ... } selects all <h1> elements on your webpage.

CSS

```
h1 {
  color: #333; /* Sets the text color to dark gray */
  font-size: 2em; /* Increases the font size */
}
```

- **Class Selector:** Targets elements with a specific CSS class applied using the class attribute in HTML. For example, .heading-special { ... } selects all elements with the class heading-special.

HTML

```
<h1 class="heading-special">This heading has special styling!</h1>
```

CSS

```
.heading-special {
  color: red; /* Sets the text color to red */

  text-shadow: 2px 2px 5px #ccc; /* Adds a subtle text
shadow */

}
```

- **ID Selector:** Targets a unique element using the id attribute in HTML. The id attribute should be unique on the webpage. For example, #main-banner { ... } selects the element with the ID main-banner.

HTML

```
<div id="main-banner">This is the main banner of the
webpage.</div>
```

CSS

```
#main-banner {
    background-color: #f0f0f0; /* Sets the background
color */
    padding: 20px; /* Adds padding around the content */
}
```

These are just a few basic selectors. As you progress, you'll

discover more advanced selectors to target elements with

greater precision.

4.3 Styling Text, Colors, and Backgrounds

CSS provides a vast array of properties to control the visual appearance of your webpage elements. Here are some commonly used properties:

- **Text Properties:**
  - color: Defines the text color of the element.
  - font-family: Specifies the font family to be used for the text.
  - font-size: Sets the size of the text.
  - font-weight: Controls the boldness of the text (e.g., font-weight: bold;).
- **Color Properties:**
  - background-color: Sets the background color of the element.
  - border-color: Defines the color of the element's border.

CSS

```
p {
  color: #666; /* Sets paragraph text color to a light gray */
  font-family: Arial, sans-serif; /* Uses Arial or a similar font */
  font-size: 16px; /* Sets the font size to 16 pixels */
}

.special-box {
  background-color: #f5f5f5; /* Light gray background for a special box */
  border: 1px solid #ccc; /* Adds a 1px solid gray border */
}
```

- **Background Properties:**
  - background-image: Sets an image as the background of the element.
  - background-repeat: Controls how the background image is repeated within the element. Options include repeat (repeats the

image), no-repeat (displays the image only once), and repeat-x or repeat-y (repeats the image only horizontally or vertically).

- ○ background-position: Defines the position of the background image within the element.

Here's an example with a background image:

CSS

```
body {
    background-image: url("background.jpg"); /* Sets the background image */
    background-repeat: repeat; /* Repeats the background image */
    background-position: center; /* Centers the background image */
}
```

These are just a few examples. Experimenting with these properties allows you to create a visually appealing and user-friendly webpage.

4.4 Applying Layouts with CSS

CSS offers various ways to control the layout of your webpage elements. Here's a glimpse into some popular approaches:

- **The Box Model:** Every HTML element can be visualized as a box with content, padding, border, and margin. CSS properties allow you to manipulate these aspects to control the spacing and positioning of elements.

CSS

```css
.content-box {
    padding: 20px; /* Adds 20px padding around the content */
    border: 1px solid #ddd; /* Adds a 1px solid light gray border */
    margin: 10px; /* Adds 10px margin around the box */
}
```

- **Float Layout:** This technique allows elements to "float" to the left or right of their container, enabling you to create side-by-side layouts with text wrapping around images or other elements.

HTML

```
<div class="container">
    <img src="image.jpg" alt="Image" style="float: left; width: 200px;">
    <p>This is some text that wraps around the image on the right.</p>
</div>
```

Note: Float layouts can be tricky to manage for complex layouts. Consider using more modern approaches like Flexbox or Grid for better control and responsiveness.

- **Flexbox (Flexible Box Layout):** This powerful layout model allows you to arrange elements horizontally or vertically with more control over alignment, spacing, and resizing. Flexbox offers greater flexibility and responsiveness compared to float layouts.

- **Grid Layout:** This approach provides a grid-based

system for positioning elements. You can define rows and columns and place elements within those grid cells, creating complex and responsive layouts.

While Flexbox and Grid are beyond the scope of this introductory chapter, exploring these techniques will open doors to creating modern and adaptable web page layouts.

By delving into CSS, you've unlocked the power to transform your basic HTML structure into visually appealing and well-designed webpages. Remember, practice and experimentation are key to mastering CSS. Play around with selectors, properties, and layout techniques to create unique and user-friendly web experiences.

CHAPTER 5

MASTERING CSS STYLES

we'll delve deeper into mastering CSS styles, covering advanced techniques for borders, margins, padding, fonts, images, selectors, and responsive design.

5.1 Borders, Margins, and Padding

We briefly touched upon these concepts in Chapter 4. Now, let's explore them in more detail:

- **The Box Model:** Recall that every HTML element can be visualized as a box with four key components:
  - **Content:** The actual content within the element (text, images, etc.).
  - **Padding:** The space between the content and

the border.

- ○ **Border:** The decorative line around the element (optional).

- ○ **Margin:** The space outside the border of the element.

CSS

```
.box {
    padding: 10px; /* Adds 10px padding around the content */
    border: 2px solid #ccc; /* Creates a 2px solid light gray border */
    margin: 15px; /* Adds 15px margin around the box */
}
```

- • **Border Styles:** CSS offers various border styles beyond the basic solid line. You can define styles like dotted, dashed, double, or even create custom borders with images.

CSS

```
.special-box {
    border: 5px dashed #f00; /* Creates a 5px dashed red border */
}
```

- **Border Shorthand:** You can define all border properties (style, width, color) in a single shorthand declaration.

CSS

```
.box {
  border: 1px solid #ddd; /* Equivalent to the previous example */
}
```

- **Margin Shorthand:** Similar to borders, margins can be defined using a shorthand property.

CSS

```
.box {
  margin: 10px 20px; /* Sets 10px margin on top and bottom, 20px on left and right */
}
```

By mastering these properties, you can create well-structured and visually appealing web page layouts.

5.2 Working with Fonts and Images in CSS

Chapter 4 introduced basic font and image properties. Now, let's explore some advanced techniques:

- **Font Properties:**

  - font-family: This property allows you to specify a list of font families, separated by commas. If the user's browser doesn't have the first font, it will try the subsequent fonts in the list.

  - font-style: Controls the style of the font (e.g., font-style: italic;).

  - text-decoration: Defines text decorations like underline, overline, or line-through.

CSS

```
h1 {
    font-family: "Open Sans", Arial, sans-serif; /* Uses
Open Sans if available, falls back to Arial or a similar font
*/
    font-style: italic; /* Sets the heading text to italic */
}

a {
    text-decoration: none; /* Removes underline from links
```

by default */

    text-decoration: underline hover; /* Underline links only on hover */

  }

- **Image Properties:**

  - background-size: Controls the size and positioning of a background image. You can set it to cover (fill the entire container), contain (fit the image within the container while maintaining aspect ratio), or specific pixel dimensions.

  - background-position: Defines the placement of the background image within the element. You can use percentages or keywords like top, center, bottom, left, or right.

CSS

.banner {

  background-image: url("banner.jpg");

  background-size: cover; /* Fills the container with the background image */

background-position: center; /* Centers the background image */

}

These properties offer more control over how fonts and images are displayed on your webpage.

5.3 Advanced Selectors for Precise Styling

Now, let's explore some advanced techniques for targeting specific elements:

- **Descendant Selector:** Targets elements that are nested within another element. For example, div p { ... } selects all <p> elements that are descendants of a <div> element.

HTML

```
<div class="content">
    <p>This is a paragraph inside a div with class "content".</p>
    </div>
```

CSS

```
div.content p {
  color: blue; /* Makes all paragraphs within the div with
class "content" blue */
```

- **Child Selector:** Targets elements that are directly nested within another element, but not any further nested elements. You can use the > symbol to specify a child relationship.

HTML

```
<ul>
  <li>Item 1</li>
  <li class="special">Item 2 (special)</li>
</ul>
```

CSS

```
ul > li.special {
  font-weight: bold; /* Makes only the "special" list item
bold */
}
```

- **Pseudo-Classes:** These are special selectors that target elements based on a particular state or condition. Here are some common examples:

  - :hover: Applies styles when the user hovers

over an element with the mouse (e.g., a:hover { color: red; } makes links turn red on hover).

- :active: Applies styles when the user clicks and holds an element (e.g., button:active { background-color: #ddd; }).

- :focus: Applies styles when an element receives focus (e.g., for accessibility, you can style the outline of a focused input field).

- **Pseudo-Elements:** These target specific parts of an element, like the first letter or content before/after an element.

  - ::first-letter: Targets the first letter of an element and allows for styling it differently (e.g., h1::first-letter { text-transform: uppercase; } makes the first letter of all headings uppercase).

  - ::before and ::after: Insert content before or after an element, respectively. This can be useful for creating decorative elements or pseudo-content.

By mastering these advanced selectors, you can achieve a high level of precision in your CSS styling, targeting specific elements and applying styles based on various conditions.

5.4 Responsive Design: Building for Different Screens

In today's world, users access webpages from various devices – desktops, laptops, tablets, and smartphones. Responsive design ensures your webpage adapts its layout to different screen sizes, providing an optimal viewing experience on any device.

Here are some core concepts of responsive design:

- **Media Queries:** These CSS queries allow you to define styles based on specific media types (like screen size) or device orientations. You can use media queries to adjust font sizes, layouts, and image sizes for different screen sizes.

CSS

```
@media only screen and (max-width: 768px) {
  /* Styles for screens less than 768px wide (e.g., tablets)
*/
  h1 {
    font-size: 1.5em; /* Reduce heading size for smaller
screens */
  }
  .content {
    padding: 10px; /* Adjust padding for better layout on
tablets */
  }
}

@media only screen and (max-width: 480px) {
  /* Styles for screens less than 480px wide (e.g.,
smartphones) */
  img {
    width: 100%; /* Make images responsive on small
screens */
  }
}
```

- **Flexible Units:** Using flexible units like em, rem, vw, and vh allows elements to scale based on the viewport size or parent element size. This makes your layout more adaptable to different screen resolutions.

By incorporating responsive design principles, you can ensure your webpages are user-friendly and visually appealing across a wide range of devices.

CHAPTER 6

Bringing Your Webpage to Life with JavaScript

So far, you've built the foundation of your webpage structure with HTML and styled it visually with CSS. Now, it's time to add the magic touch – interactivity! JavaScript is a powerful scripting language that breathes life into your webpages, making them dynamic and responsive to user actions.

6.1 What is JavaScript and What Can it Do?

Imagine your webpage as a static brochure. JavaScript transforms it into an engaging experience, allowing users to interact with elements, provide input, and see dynamic content updates. Here are some examples of what JavaScript can do:

- **Respond to User Events:** JavaScript can detect user

actions like clicks, mouse hovers, key presses, and form submissions. Based on these events, it can trigger specific behaviors on the webpage.

- **Manipulate the DOM (Document Object Model):** JavaScript can access and modify the HTML content and CSS styles of your webpage dynamically. This allows you to update text, change element attributes, and create animations.

- **Validate User Input:** JavaScript can ensure users enter data in the correct format before submitting forms, improving the user experience and data integrity.

- **Create Dynamic Content:** JavaScript can fetch data from external sources (like databases or APIs) and display it on your webpage, making your content more interactive and up-to-date.

By incorporating JavaScript, you can create webpages that are more engaging, user-friendly, and dynamic.

6.2 The Basics of JavaScript Syntax

JavaScript has its own syntax, similar to other programming languages. Here's a glimpse into the fundamentals:

- **Variables:** These store data that can be used throughout your JavaScript code. Variables are declared using the var, let, or const keywords, followed by the variable name and an optional assignment value.

JavaScript

```
var message = "Hello, world!"; // Declares a variable named "message" with the value "Hello, world!"
let age = 25; // Another way to declare variables (introduced in ES6)
const PI = 3.14159; // Constant value that cannot be changed
```

- **Data Types:** JavaScript supports various data types to represent different kinds of information:

- ○ string: Text data enclosed in quotes (e.g., "This is a string").

- ○ number: Numerical data (e.g., 10, 3.14).

- ○ boolean: True or false values.

- ○ array: An ordered list of items within square brackets (e.g., ["apple", "banana", "cherry"]).

- ○ object: A collection of key-value pairs to store complex data structures (e.g., { name: "John", age: 30 }).

- **Comments:** Adding comments within your code improves readability and explains what your code does. Comments are ignored by the browser when running the script.

JavaScript

```
// This is a single-line comment
/* This is a multi-line comment */
```

- **Operators:** JavaScript provides various operators to perform calculations, comparisons, and logical operations. These include arithmetic operators (+, -, *, /), comparison operators (==, !=, <, >), and logical operators (&&, ||, !).

JavaScript

```
var sum = 10 + 5; // Assigns the sum of 10 and 5 to the variable "sum"
if (age >= 18) { // Checks if "age" is greater than or equal to 18
    console.log("You are eligible.");
}
```

These are just the fundamental building blocks. As you progress, you'll explore more advanced concepts like functions, control flow statements, and object-oriented programming principles.

6.3 Adding Interactivity with Events and Functions

JavaScript allows you to capture user interactions (events)

and execute specific code (functions) in response to those events.

- **Events:** These are user actions or browser occurrences that trigger JavaScript code. Common events include click, mouseover, submit, and load.

HTML

```
<button onclick="showAlert()">Click me!</button>
```

JavaScript

```
function showAlert() {
  alert("You clicked the button!");
}
```

In this example, clicking the button triggers the onclick event, which calls the showAlert() function. This function displays an alert message to the user.

- **Functions:** These are reusable blocks of code that perform specific tasks. Functions are defined using the function keyword, followed by the function name, parameters (optional), and the code block to be executed.

JavaScript

```javascript
function greetUser(name) {
  alert("Hello, " + name + "!");
}
```

- **Function Parameters and Arguments:** Functions can accept input values called parameters. When calling the function, you provide arguments (actual values) that are passed to the function's parameters.

In the previous example, the greetUser function takes a parameter named name. When calling the function, you provide an argument (e.g., greetUser("Alice")) which is assigned to the name parameter within the function.

- **Event Listeners:** A more modern approach for handling events is to use event listeners. These allow you to attach specific functions to listen for events on particular HTML elements.

HTML

```
<button id="myButton">Click me!</button>
```

JavaScript

```
var button = document.getElementById("myButton");

button.addEventListener("click", function() {
  alert("You clicked the button!");
});
```

Here, we use document.getElementById to access the button element and then attach an event listener for the click event. The provided function is executed whenever the button is clicked.

By mastering events and functions, you can create dynamic and interactive webpages that respond to user actions in meaningful ways.

6.4 Building Dynamic Content with JavaScript

JavaScript not only reacts to user interactions but can also manipulate the content and structure of your webpage dynamically. Here are some ways to achieve this:

- **Accessing and Modifying the DOM:** JavaScript can access and modify the Document Object Model (DOM), which represents the HTML structure of your webpage. You can use methods like getElementById, getElementsByClassName, and querySelector to target specific elements and then modify their content using properties like innerHTML or textContent.

HTML

```
<p id="message">This is a message.</p>
```

JavaScript

```
var messageElement = document.getElementById("message");
messageElement.innerHTML = "The message has been updated!";
```

- **Creating and Removing Elements:** JavaScript can dynamically create new HTML elements and add them to the DOM. You can also remove existing elements as needed.

JavaScript

```
var newElement = document.createElement("p");
newElement.textContent = "This is a new paragraph.";

document.body.appendChild(newElement);
```

- **AJAX (Asynchronous JavaScript and XML):** This technique allows JavaScript to communicate with a web server and retrieve data asynchronously (without reloading the entire page). This retrieved data can then be used to update the webpage content dynamically.

These capabilities empower you to create rich and interactive web experiences that adapt and update based on user actions or external data.

JavaScript unlocks a new level of interactivity and dynamism for your webpages. By understanding its core concepts, events, functions, and DOM manipulation techniques, you can create engaging user experiences and transform your static webpages into dynamic applications. In the next chapter, we'll explore how to take your web development skills even further by delving into the world of server-side scripting languages!

CHAPTER 7

JavaScript for User Interaction

Let's delve deeper into specific ways JavaScript enhances user interaction through forms, animations, dynamic elements, and interactive components.

7.1 Working with Forms and User Input

HTML forms allow users to submit information. JavaScript empowers you to validate, process, and handle user input effectively.

- **Form Validation:** JavaScript can ensure users enter data in the correct format before submitting the form. This improves data integrity and user experience.

HTML

```html
<form id="myForm">
  <label for="name">Name:</label>
  <input type="text" id="name" name="name" required>
  <button type="submit">Submit</button>
</form>
```

JavaScript

```javascript
var form = document.getElementById("myForm");

form.addEventListener("submit", function(event) {
  var name = document.getElementById("name").value;
  if (name === "") {
    alert("Please enter your name!");
        event.preventDefault(); // Prevents the form from submitting
  }
});
```

In this example, JavaScript checks if the name field is empty before submission. If so, it displays an alert message and prevents the form from submitting.

- **Processing Form Data:** After successful validation, JavaScript can access the submitted data and process it further. You can extract form data using the value property of input elements and then handle it using logic or send it to a server for processing.

JavaScript

```
function handleFormSubmit(event) {
  var name = document.getElementById("name").value;
  var email = document.getElementById("email").value;

  // Process form data (e.g., send it to a server using AJAX)
  console.log("Name:", name, "Email:", email);

  event.preventDefault();
}
```

- **AJAX and Form Submission:** Using AJAX, JavaScript can submit form data to a server asynchronously without reloading the entire page. This provides a smoother user experience.

By mastering form validation and processing, you can ensure accurate data collection and efficient interactions with your webpages.

7.2 Creating Animations and Transitions

Animations and smooth transitions can enhance user experience and make your webpage more visually engaging. JavaScript offers various ways to achieve these effects:

- **CSS Animations:** JavaScript can trigger CSS animations defined in your stylesheet. By manipulating the animation-name and animation-play-state properties of elements, you can control the animation playback.

HTML

```
<div class="animated-box">This box will animate!</div>
```

CSS

```
.animated-box {
  animation: myAnimation 2s ease-in-out infinite;
}

@keyframes myAnimation {
  from { transform: scale(1); }
  to { transform: scale(1.2); }
}
```

JavaScript

```javascript
var box = document.querySelector(".animated-box");

box.addEventListener("click", function() {
    box.style.animationPlayState = "running"; // Start the animation
});
```

- **JavaScript Libraries:** Several JavaScript libraries like jQuery or Anime.js provide powerful animation functionalities. These libraries offer pre-built animations and simplify animation creation, making complex effects more manageable.

JavaScript

```javascript
$("#myElement").animate({ opacity: 0.5 }, 1000); // Fade out the element in 1 second using jQuery
```

By incorporating animations and transitions, you can add visual interest and improve the overall user experience of your webpages.

7.3 JavaScript for Dynamic Web Page Elements

As discussed in Chapter 6, JavaScript can manipulate the DOM and dynamically modify the content and structure of your webpage. Here are some advanced applications:

- **Creating Interactive Content:** JavaScript allows you to create content that updates based on user interactions or external data. For example, you can implement image galleries with navigation controls or dynamically create product listings based on user selections.

JavaScript

```
function showProductDetails(productId) {
  // Fetch product data from a server (using AJAX)
  // Update the webpage content with product details
}
```

- **Updating Content with AJAX:** By fetching data from a server asynchronously using AJAX, you can update specific parts of your webpage without reloading the entire page. This improves performance and responsiveness.

JavaScript

```
function updateNewsFeed() {
    // Fetch latest news articles from a server
    // Create HTML elements for each news article
    // Add the new content to the webpage
}
```

These techniques empower you to create dynamic and interactive web experiences that adapt based on user actions and external data.

7.4 Building Popups, Modals, and Accordions

JavaScript's ability to manipulate the DOM and respond to user events opens doors to creating interactive UI components that enhance user experience. Here, we'll explore popups, modals, and accordions.

- **Popups:** These are separate windows that appear on top of the main webpage content. They can be used for various purposes, such as displaying login forms, notifications, or promotional messages.

Here's a basic example of a popup:

HTML

```html
<div id="popup" class="hidden">
 <h2>Welcome!</h2>
 <p>This is a sample popup message.</p>
 <button id="closePopup">Close</button>
</div>

<button id="openPopup">Open Popup</button>
```

CSS

```css
#popup {
  background-color: #fff;
  padding: 20px;
  border: 1px solid #ccc;
   position: fixed; /* Positions the popup on top of the
main content */
  top: 50%; /* Centers the popup vertically */
  left: 50%; /* Centers the popup horizontally */
   transform: translate(-50%, -50%); /* More precise
centering */
  display: none; /* Initially hide the popup */
```

```
}
```

JavaScript

```javascript
var popup = document.getElementById("popup");
var openPopupBtn = document.getElementById("openPopup");
var closePopupBtn = document.getElementById("closePopup");

openPopupBtn.addEventListener("click", function() {
    popup.classList.remove("hidden"); // Remove the hidden class to show the popup
});

closePopupBtn.addEventListener("click", function() {
    popup.classList.add("hidden"); // Add the hidden class to hide the popup
});
```

In this example, clicking the "Open Popup" button removes the "hidden" class from the popup element, making it visible. Clicking the "Close" button within the popup adds the "hidden" class back, hiding the popup.

- **Modals:** Similar to popups, modals are typically larger windows that appear on top of the main content, often with a dimmed background to focus user attention. They are commonly used for login forms, product details, or confirmation messages.

Modals often employ a slightly more complex structure to handle background dimming and user interaction outside the modal. Libraries like Bootstrap provide pre-built modal components for easier implementation.

- **Accordions:** These are interactive elements that allow users to expand and collapse sections of content. They are useful for presenting large amounts of information in an organized and space-saving way.

Here's a simplified example of an accordion:

HTML

```html
<div class="accordion">
  <div class="accordion-item">
    <h3 class="accordion-header">Section 1</h3>
      <div class="accordion-content">This is the content
for section 1.</div>
  </div>
  <div class="accordion-item">
    <h3 class="accordion-header">Section 2</h3>
      <div class="accordion-content">This is the content
for section 2.</div>
  </div>
</div>
```

CSS

```css
.accordion {
  border: 1px solid #ddd;
}

.accordion-item {
  border-bottom: 1px solid #ddd;
}

.accordion-header {
  cursor: pointer;
  padding: 10px;
}

.accordion-content {
  padding: 10px;
  display: none; /* Initially hide the content */
```

```
}

.accordion-item.active .accordion-content {
  display: block; /* Show content for active item */
}
```

JavaScript

```
var accordionItems =
document.querySelectorAll(".accordion-item");

accordionItems.forEach(function(item) {
  var header = item.querySelector(".accordion-header");

  header.addEventListener("click", function() {
    var content =
item.querySelector(".accordion-content");
    item.classList.toggle("active"); // Toggle active class
for expansion/collapse
    content.classList.toggle("show"); // Toggle display of
content
  });
});
```

In this example, clicking on the header of an accordion item toggles the "active" class for that item. The JavaScript code then adjusts the visibility of the corresponding content section based on the active state.

By incorporating these interactive elements, you can create user interfaces that are more engaging, informative, and user-friendly.

JavaScript empowers you to build dynamic and interactive webpages. By mastering techniques

By mastering techniques covered in this chapter, you can create user interfaces that are more engaging, informative, and user-friendly.

Additional Considerations:

- **Accessibility:** Ensure your interactive elements are accessible to users with disabilities. This includes providing keyboard navigation for popups and modals, and proper semantic HTML for screen readers.

- **Responsiveness:** Make sure your popups, modals, and accordions adapt to different screen sizes and devices for optimal user experience. Use media queries in your CSS to adjust layouts and styles.

- **Libraries and Frameworks:** Several JavaScript libraries and frameworks like jQuery, Bootstrap, and React offer pre-built components and functionalities for creating popups, modals, accordions, and other interactive elements. These tools can simplify development and provide a consistent design aesthetic.

These considerations help you build robust and user-friendly interactive features.

7.5 Beyond the Basics: Advanced User Interactions

JavaScript offers even more advanced techniques for user interaction:

- **Drag and Drop:** Users can drag and drop elements on the webpage to rearrange them, upload files, or create custom interactions. JavaScript libraries like Dragula or Sortable.js simplify drag-and-drop functionalities.

- **Touch Events:** In the age of touch-enabled devices, JavaScript allows you to handle user gestures like taps, swipes, and pinches for intuitive interactions.

Exploring these advanced techniques opens doors to creating highly interactive and engaging web applications.

JavaScript empowers you to build dynamic and interactive webpages that go beyond static content. By mastering the concepts covered in this chapter, you can create user interfaces that are not only visually appealing but also provide a seamless and engaging user experience.

CHAPTER 8

Beyond the Basics: Advanced Web Development

you've built a solid foundation in HTML, CSS, and JavaScript, empowering you to create basic webpages. Now, we'll venture into the exciting world of advanced web development, exploring frameworks, tools, coding best practices, and debugging techniques to take your skills to the next level.

8.1 Introduction to Frameworks and Libraries

Building complex web applications from scratch can be time-consuming. Frameworks and libraries offer pre-built code and functionalities that streamline development and promote consistency.

- **Frameworks:** These provide a more comprehensive structure for building web applications. They offer pre-defined components, routing mechanisms, data binding techniques, and other features to accelerate development. Popular frameworks include:

- **React:** A powerful JavaScript library for building user interfaces with a focus on component-based architecture.

- **Angular:** A comprehensive framework from Google, offering a wide range of features and tools for building single-page applications (SPAs).

- **Vue.js:** A lightweight and versatile framework with a focus on simplicity and ease of learning.

HTML

```
<template>
  <div>
    <h1>Hello, {{ name }}!</h1>
            <button    @click="increment">Increment
Count</button>
    <p>Count: {{ count }}</p>
  </div>
</template>
```

```
<script>
export default {
  data() {
    return {
      name: "World",
      count: 0
    };
  },
  methods: {
    increment() {
      this.count++;
    }
  }
};
</script>

<style scoped>
h1 {
  color: blue;
}
</style>
```

(This code snippet showcases a simple React component that displays a greeting and a counter)

- **Libraries:** These offer specific functionalities or utilities that can be integrated into your web application. Popular libraries include:

  - **jQuery:** A widely used JavaScript library that

simplifies DOM manipulation, event handling, and AJAX interactions.

○ **Bootstrap:** A front-end framework providing pre-built components like buttons, forms, navigation bars, and more, for faster and consistent UI development.

○ **Lodash:** A utility library offering various functions for data manipulation, arrays, and objects.

By leveraging frameworks and libraries, you can:

- **Reduce development time:** Pre-built components and functionalities save significant coding effort.

- **Improve code quality:** Frameworks often enforce coding practices and offer built-in features for better code organization and maintainability.

- **Promote consistency:** Frameworks and libraries help maintain a consistent look and feel across your application.

Choosing the right framework or library depends on your project's specific needs and complexity.

8.2 Exploring Web Development Tools and Resources

As you delve deeper into web development, a variety of tools and resources become invaluable companions:

- **Browser Developer Tools:** Every modern browser offers built-in developer tools. These provide functionalities like:

  - **Inspecting the DOM:** Visually examine the HTML structure, CSS styles, and applied JavaScript code for any element on the webpage.
  - **Debugging JavaScript:** Set breakpoints in your code, step through execution line by line, and inspect variables to identify errors.
  - **Network monitoring:** Analyze network requests made by the webpage, including

response times and content analysis.

- **Code Editors and IDEs:** A good code editor or Integrated Development Environment (IDE) can significantly enhance your development experience. Some popular options include:

  - **Visual Studio Code:** A versatile and free code editor with extensive features and plugins.
  - **WebStorm:** A powerful IDE specifically designed for web development, offering advanced features like code completion, refactoring, and debugging tools.
  - **Atom:** A customizable and open-source code editor with a large plugin ecosystem.

- **Online Resources:** The web is a treasure trove of learning materials. Here are some valuable resources to explore:

  - **MDN Web Docs:** The official documentation

from Mozilla provides detailed information on HTML, CSS, JavaScript, and web development APIs.

- ○ **W3Schools:** A comprehensive online tutorial website covering various web development technologies.
- ○ **Stack Overflow:** A question-and-answer platform for developers, where you can find solutions to common problems and learn from others.

By mastering these tools and resources, you'll streamline your development workflow, diagnose and fix problems efficiently, and stay up-to-date with the latest advancements in web development.

8.3 Best Practices for Writing Clean and Maintainable Code

As your codebase grows, writing clean and maintainable code becomes crucial. Here are some best practices to follow:

- **Meaningful Naming:** Use descriptive variable and function names that clearly reflect their purpose. This improves code readability and understanding for yourself and others who might collaborate on the project.

JavaScript

```javascript
// Descriptive variable name
var userName = document.getElementById("user-name");

// Descriptive function name
function updateProductQuantity(productId, newQuantity) {
  // ... function logic ...
}
```

- **Code Formatting:** Consistent indentation, spacing, and line breaks make your code visually appealing and easier to read. Many code editors and IDEs offer auto-formatting options to enforce consistent style.

JavaScript

```
// Well-formatted code

if (userAge >= 18) {
  console.log("User is eligible.");
} else {
  console.log("User is not eligible.");
}

// Poorly formatted code (hard to read)
if(userAge>=18)console.log("User    is    eligible.")else
console.log("User is not eligible.")
```

- **Commenting:** Add clear and concise comments to explain complex logic or non-obvious code sections. Comments improve code maintainability and understanding for future reference.

JavaScript

```
// Function with comments explaining its purpose and
```

parameters

```
function calculateTotalPrice(price, quantity, discount) {
  // ... calculation logic ...

  // Explain the purpose of the discount calculation
  // ...

  return totalPrice;
}
```

- **Modularization:** Break down your code into smaller, reusable functions with well-defined responsibilities. This promotes code reusability, improves maintainability, and makes your code easier to test.

JavaScript

```
// Separate function for calculating the discount

function calculateDiscount(price, discountRate) {
  return price * discountRate;
}

function calculateTotalPrice(price, quantity) {
```

```
var discount = calculateDiscount(price, 0.1); // Apply a
10% discount
    var totalPrice = price * quantity - discount;
    return totalPrice;

}
```

- **Error Handling:** Implement proper error handling mechanisms to gracefully handle unexpected situations and prevent your application from crashing. Use try...catch blocks or conditional checks to anticipate potential errors and provide informative feedback to the user.

JavaScript

```
try {
    var age = parseInt(userInput); // Attempt to convert
user input to a number
    if (isNaN(age)) {
        throw new Error("Invalid age format."); // Throw an
error if conversion fails
    }
    // ... process valid age ...
} catch (error) {
    console.error("Error:", error.message);
    alert("Please enter a valid age."); // Inform the user
about the error
```

```
}
```

By following these best practices, you'll write code that is not only functional but also easy to understand, maintain, and modify in the future.

8.4 Debugging Techniques for Troubleshooting Your Code

Even the most experienced developers encounter bugs and errors in their code. Mastering debugging techniques empowers you to identify and fix these issues efficiently.

- **Console Logging:** The browser console is your best friend for debugging. Use console.log statements to print variable values, function execution flow, or error messages at different points in your code.

JavaScript

```
console.log("User name:", userName);
console.log("Before function call:", productQuantity);

updateProductQuantity(productId, newQuantity);
```

```
console.log("After function call:", productQuantity);
```

- **Browser Developer Tools:** As mentioned earlier, browser developer tools offer functionalities like setting breakpoints in your code. This allows you to pause code execution at specific points, inspect variables, and step through the code line by line to pinpoint the exact location of an error.

- **Rubber Duck Debugging:** Sometimes, explaining your code to an imaginary listener (like a rubber duck) can help you identify logical flaws or errors in your thought process. By verbalizing your approach, you might spot mistakes you previously overlooked.

- **Online Resources and Forums:** The web development community is vast and supportive. If you're stuck on a particularly challenging bug, don't hesitate to search online forums like Stack Overflow for similar issues or explanations. Clearly describe your problem and the code snippet causing the issue to get help from experienced developers.

Remember, debugging is an iterative process. By methodically applying these techniques and leveraging available resources, you'll become more efficient at troubleshooting and resolving issues in your code.

This chapter has equipped you with valuable knowledge for venturing beyond the basics of web development. By understanding frameworks and libraries, utilizing developer tools, adhering to best practices, and mastering debugging techniques, you'll be well on your way to building complex, interactive, and maintainable web applications.

The journey of web development is a continuous learning process. Embrace new technologies, explore innovative solutions, and keep practicing to refine your skills.

CHAPTER 9

Congratulations! You've built a fantastic website using HTML, CSS, and JavaScript. Now, it's time to share your creation with the world. This chapter will guide you through the process of deploying your website, making it accessible on the internet.

9.1 Choosing a Web Hosting Platform

A web hosting platform provides the storage space and infrastructure required to run your website. It's essentially the "home" for your website's files, making them accessible to users through the internet. Here are some factors to consider when choosing a web hosting platform:

- **Shared Hosting:** This is the most affordable option,

where your website shares server resources with other websites. It's a good starting point for personal websites or those with low traffic.

- **Virtual Private Server (VPS):** Offers more dedicated resources than shared hosting, providing better performance and control over your server environment. Suitable for websites with moderate traffic or requiring more customization.

- **Cloud Hosting:** Leverages cloud computing technology, offering scalability and flexibility. You only pay for the resources you use, making it a good option for websites with fluctuating traffic.

- **Dedicated Hosting:** Provides the highest level of control and resources. You have an entire server dedicated to your website, ideal for high-traffic websites or those requiring maximum security.

Here are some popular web hosting providers to consider:

- Bluehost
- HostGator

- GoDaddy

- DreamHost

- SiteGround

These providers offer various hosting plans with different features and pricing options. Carefully evaluate your website's needs and choose a plan that best suits your budget and traffic expectations.

9.2 Uploading Your Files to the Server

Once you've chosen a web hosting provider, you'll need to upload your website's files to their server. Most providers offer a File Transfer Protocol (FTP) client or a web-based file manager to facilitate this process.

- **FTP Clients:** These are dedicated software applications specifically designed for uploading and managing files on a server. Popular options include FileZilla and Cyberduck.

- **Web-based File Managers:** Many web hosting providers offer a user-friendly web interface for managing your website's files directly through your browser. This eliminates the need for a separate FTP client.

Here's a general overview of the upload process:

1. **Gather your website files:** Ensure you have all the necessary files and folders that make up your website, including HTML pages, CSS stylesheets, JavaScript files, and any images or media.

2. **Connect to your server:** Use your FTP client or web-based file manager to connect to your web hosting provider's server using the provided credentials (username, password, and server address).

3. **Upload your files:** Navigate to the appropriate directory on the server, typically the public_html or www folder. Upload all your website's files and

folders to this location.

4. **Verify file permissions:** Ensure your files have the correct permissions for the web server to access them properly. Some servers might require specific permissions for certain files (e.g., scripts needing executable permissions).

Once you've uploaded your files, your website should be accessible on the internet using the web address (URL) provided by your hosting provider.

9.3 Domain Names and Website Registration

While your website files reside on the server, users need a memorable and user-friendly address to access it. This is where domain names come in.

- **Domain Name:** This is the human-readable address used to access your website (e.g., [invalid URL removed]). It serves as your website's unique identifier on the internet.

You can purchase a domain name from a domain registrar like Google Domains, Namecheap, or GoDaddy. The registration process typically involves searching for an available domain name, selecting a domain extension (.com, .org, .net, etc.), and completing the purchase.

Once you've purchased a domain name, you'll need to configure it to point to your web hosting server. This involves editing the domain name's DNS (Domain Name System) records to direct users to the server where your website files are located. Your web hosting provider will usually guide you through this configuration process.

9.4 Maintaining and Updating Your Website

Your website is not a static entity. It requires ongoing maintenance and updates to ensure smooth operation, security, and fresh content. Here are some key aspects of website maintenance:

- **Content Updates:** Keep your website content fresh

and up-to-date. Regularly add new information, blog posts, or product offerings to maintain user engagement.

- **Security Updates:** Software updates for your CMS (Content Management System) or any plugins used on your website are crucial. These updates often address security vulnerabilities and ensure your website remains protected from potential threats.

- **Backups:** Regularly create backups of your website's files and database (if applicable). This ensures you have a restore point in case of unexpected issues like server crashes or accidental data loss.

- **Monitoring and Analytics:** Track website traffic, user behavior, and performance metrics using analytics tools like Google Analytics. This data can provide valuable insights for improving your website's user experience and overall effectiveness.

- **Broken Link Checking:** Periodically check for broken links on your website. These can occur due to changes in URLs or removed pages. Fixing broken links ensures a smooth user experience and avoids frustrating users with dead ends.

Here are some additional tips for maintaining your website:

- **Test Updates Thoroughly:** Before deploying any major updates or changes to your live website, thoroughly test them on a development or staging server. This helps identify and fix any potential issues before they impact your live site.
- **Stay Informed:** The web development landscape is constantly evolving. Keep yourself informed about new technologies, trends, and security best practices to ensure your website stays up-to-date and secure.

By following these practices, you can maintain a healthy and well-functioning website that continues to provide value to your visitors.

9.5 Going Beyond Basic Deployment

For more complex websites or web applications, deployment might involve additional considerations:

- **Database Management:** If your website relies on a database to store information (e.g., user accounts, product data), you'll need to set up and manage a database on your web hosting server. Popular database management systems include MySQL, PostgreSQL, and MongoDB.

- **Server-side Scripting:** While HTML, CSS, and JavaScript primarily focus on the presentation layer, websites often require server-side scripting languages like PHP, Python, or Node.js to handle tasks like processing user input, interacting with databases, or generating dynamic content.

- **Deployment Automation:** For larger projects with frequent updates, deploying website changes manually can become cumbersome. Tools and techniques like continuous integration/continuous delivery (CI/CD) can automate the deployment process, ensuring consistency and efficiency.

These advanced topics are beyond the scope of this introductory guide but serve as stepping stones for further exploration as you delve deeper into web development.

Congratulations! You've successfully navigated the exciting world of web development, from learning the fundamentals of HTML, CSS, and JavaScript to deploying your very own website. Remember, this is just the beginning of your journey. Keep practicing, experimenting, and exploring new technologies to create even more engaging and interactive web experiences. The future of the web is bright, and with your newfound skills, you're well on your way to becoming a part of it!

CHAPTER 10

THE FUTURE OF WEB DEVELOPMENT

The web development landscape is constantly evolving, with new technologies and trends emerging at a rapid pace. This chapter will explore what the future holds for web development, discuss the importance of accessibility and inclusivity, and guide you on potential career paths and your continuous learning journey.

10.1 Emerging Trends and Technologies

Here are some exciting trends and technologies shaping the future of web development:

- **Progressive Web Apps (PWAs):** PWAs blur the lines between websites and native apps. They offer functionalities like offline access, push notifications, and home screen installation, providing an app-like experience accessible through a web browser.

JavaScript

```
// Service worker registration for offline functionality
(example)
  if ('serviceWorker' in navigator) {
    window.addEventListener('load', () => {
    navigator.serviceWorker.register('/service-worker.js')
      .then(registration => {
              console.log('Service worker registered: ',
registration.scope);
      })
      .catch(registrationError => {
          console.log('Service worker registration failed: ',
registrationError);
      });
    });
  }
```

- **Single-Page Applications (SPAs):** SPAs provide a seamless user experience by loading a single HTML page and dynamically updating content using JavaScript. This creates a faster and more responsive user experience.

- **Artificial Intelligence (AI) and Machine Learning**

(ML): AI and ML are finding their way into web development. Chatbots powered by AI can handle user queries, while machine learning algorithms can personalize content recommendations or optimize website performance.

- **Voice Search Optimization:** As voice assistants and smart speakers become more prevalent, websites need to be optimized for voice search. This includes using natural language and focusing on long-tail keywords to ensure users can find your website through voice queries.

- **Internet of Things (IoT):** The growing number of internet-connected devices (IoT) is opening doors for new web development opportunities. Websites can interact with and control these devices, creating a more interconnected and automated world.

- **Blockchain Technology:** While still in its early

stages, blockchain technology has the potential to revolutionize web development. It can enable secure and transparent data storage and transactions, paving the way for new decentralized applications.

Staying informed about these trends will equip you to build future-proof web applications that leverage the latest advancements in technology.

10.2 Building for Accessibility and Inclusivity

Accessibility is the principle of ensuring that websites are usable by everyone, regardless of their abilities. Here's why accessibility matters:

- **Ethical Responsibility:** Everyone deserves equal access to information and opportunities on the web. Building accessible websites promotes inclusivity and ensures everyone can benefit from your creation.

- **Wider Audience Reach:** By making your website

accessible, you open it up to a broader audience, potentially increasing traffic and engagement.

- **Legal Requirements:** Many countries have regulations mandating a certain level of accessibility for websites, particularly those associated with government services or public institutions.

Here are some key principles for building accessible websites:

- **Semantic HTML:** Use HTML elements according to their semantic meaning (headings, paragraphs, lists, etc.) This helps screen readers and assistive technologies understand the structure and content of your website.

- **Alternative Text (Alt Text):** Provide descriptive alt text for images to convey their meaning to users who cannot see them. This is crucial for visually impaired users.

- **Keyboard Navigation:** Ensure your website is fully navigable using just the keyboard. This caters to users who rely on assistive technologies or have difficulty using a mouse.

- **Color Contrast:** Maintain sufficient color contrast between text and background to ensure readability for users with visual impairments.

- **Clear and Concise Language:** Use clear and concise language that is easy to understand for users with varying cognitive abilities.

By following these guidelines, you can create websites that are inclusive and accessible to a broader audience.

10.3 Career Paths in Web Development

The web development field offers a diverse range of career paths to explore, each with its unique focus and skillset requirements. Here are some popular options:

- **Front-End Developer:** Focuses on the user-facing side of websites, responsible for building the visual elements, layout, and interactivity using HTML,

CSS, and JavaScript.

- **Back-End Developer:** Works on the server-side of web applications, writing code that handles data processing, database interactions, and server logic using languages like PHP, Python, or Node.js.

- **Full-Stack Developer:** Possesses a broad skillset encompassing both front-end and back-end development, capable of working on all aspects of a web application.

- **Web Designer (continued):** Creating mockups, wireframes, and user interfaces (UIs) that are not only aesthetically pleasing but also user-friendly and intuitive.

- **Content Management System (CMS) Developer:** Specializes in developing and customizing content management systems (CMS) like WordPress or Drupal, allowing non-technical users to easily create and manage website content.

- **Web Security Engineer:** Focuses on securing web applications and websites from cyberattacks and vulnerabilities. This role requires a strong understanding of security best practices and penetration testing techniques.

The path you choose will depend on your interests, skills, and career goals. Here are some tips for navigating your web development career:

- **Build a Strong Portfolio:** Showcase your skills and creativity by building personal projects and contributing to open-source projects. A strong portfolio is essential for landing your dream web development job.

- **Stay Updated:** The web development landscape is constantly evolving. Continuously learn new technologies, frameworks, and best practices to stay relevant and competitive.

- **Network and Connect:** Connect with other web developers, attend meetups and conferences, and participate in online communities. Networking can help you learn from others, discover new opportunities, and build a strong professional network.

10.4 Continuing Your Learning Journey

Your web development journey doesn't end here. The key to success in this field is continuous learning and exploration. Here are some resources to fuel your learning:

- **Online Courses and Tutorials:** Numerous online platforms like Coursera, Udemy, and edX offer comprehensive web development courses and tutorials for all skill levels.

- **Books and Articles:** Stay updated with the latest trends and best practices by reading books and articles written by industry experts.

- **Web Development Blogs and Podcasts:** Subscribe to popular web development blogs and podcasts to get insights, tips, and industry news from experienced developers.

- **Contribute to Open-Source Projects:** Contributing

to open-source projects is a fantastic way to gain practical experience, learn from other developers, and build your portfolio.

Remember, the most successful web developers are those who are passionate about learning and constantly strive to improve their skills. Embrace the challenges, experiment with new technologies, and keep building amazing things for the web!

Conclusion

This book has equipped you with the fundamental knowledge and skills to embark on your web development journey. As you delve deeper into this dynamic field, remember to embrace the ever-evolving landscape, prioritize accessibility and inclusivity, and continuously fuel your learning. The future of web development is bright, and with dedication and passion, you can be a part of shaping it.

Happy coding!

ABOUT THE AUTHOR

Writer's Bio:

 Benjamin Evans, a respected figure in the tech world, is known for his insightful commentary and analysis. With a strong educational background likely in fields such as computer science, engineering, or business, he brings a depth of knowledge to his discussions on emerging technologies and industry trends. Evans' knack for simplifying complex concepts, coupled with his innate curiosity and passion for innovation, has established him as a go-to source for understanding the dynamics of the digital landscape. Through articles, speeches, and social media, he shares his expertise and offers valuable insights into the impact of technology on society.

www.ingramcontent.com/pod-product-compliance
Lightning Source LLC
LaVergne TN
LVHW051701050326
832903LV00032B/3934